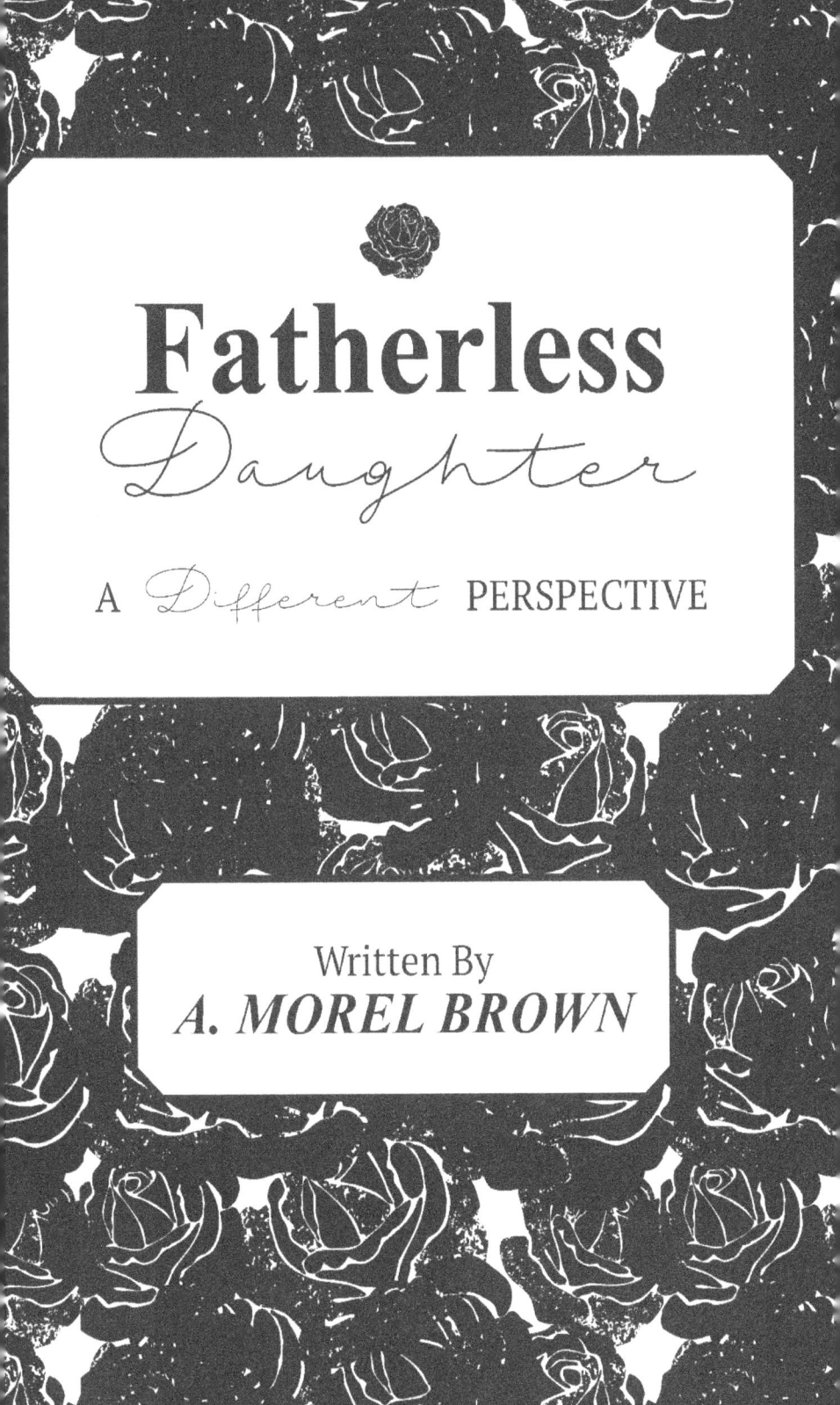

Fatherless Daughter: A Different Perspective

Copyright ©2016 by A. Morel Brown

Perfected Purpose Publishing

ISBN: 978-0-692-78168-5

All Rights Reserved. No part of this book may be reproduced in any form by any electronic or mechanical means, including information storage and retrieval systems, without permission in writing from the publisher, except by a reviewer who may quote brief passages in a review.

All Scriptures are quoted taken from the Holy Bible. Scriptures noted (NIV) are taken from the New International Version. Scriptures noted (NKJV) are taken from the New King James Version. Scriptures noted NCV are taken from the New Century Version.

Printed in the United States of America

For Speaking Engagements and bulk book orders email

info@AMorelBrown.com

Or visit www.AMorelBrown.com for more information

Dedication

This book is dedicated to all the women who were raised without a parent or who have identified with being without a parent for a period of time, more specifically without a father. I've heard people say that when you come from a "broken home," you are not expected to be successful. When speaking of success, I am not only speaking of financial success, but spiritual, mental, and physical success. When you do not have a father or father figure, you are automatically associated with negative stereotypes. Statistics show that women whose parents separated between birth and six years old experienced twice the risk of early menstruation, more than four times the risk of early sexual intercourse, and two and a half times higher risk of early pregnancy when compared to women in intact families[1]. It is important to understand that a statistic is a measurement derived from a specific population. When statisticians are seeking to gather statistics, they gather those stats from specific communities. When in specific communities, the information that is gathered cannot account for every individual experience, which means it will not apply to everyone.

The purpose of this book is to provide not only my truth, but perspectives of women who have been successful despite the obstacles that we've faced, and despite not having one of our parents; our fathers. I wanted to provide different perspectives of fatherlessness so that this book relates to more than just one situation. I hope that this book provides encouragement, inspiration, and empowerment to young and mature women who have fought the battle of feeling unable to find herself due to feeling like she is or has been missing a part of herself. I love you all with the love of Christ, and know that while

---

[1] "What We've Learned" - Growingupwithoutafather.org

you may not have a physical father, you are the Princess to a King who resides on the Throne.

Contents

Dedication v
Introduction: My Truth xiii
Chapter One: Understand The Curse… Break The Curse! 1
Chapter Two: Love And Forgiveness 9
Chapter Three: Your Past Does Not Determine Your Future 21
Chapter Four: Prioritize Your Life, Set Goals,
    And Start Early! 33
Chapter Five: Create A Vision And Edit As You Go 41
Chapter Six: Unveiling The Truth After Death 47
Chapter Seven: The Good, The Bad, And The Ugly 53
Chapter Eight: Kind Of Like A Nice Uncle 57
Chapter Nine: What Determines True Success? 69
Chapter Ten: My Father In Heaven 75
Chapter Eleven: Daddy's Girl…Still 85
Chapter Twelve: God Has Already Determined
    Your Success 93
Chapter Thirteen: I Was Always Hopeful 97
Chapter Fourteen: The Heart Of A Legacy, Mind Over
    Matter *(The Doctor's Perspective)* 103
Chapter Fifteen: You Are The Daughter Of A King 113
Acknowledgements 121
Notes 124

Fatherless

Daughter

A *Different* Perspective

A. MOREL BROWN

Introduction

My Truth

When people ask how often I have seen my father, my response is, "Out of my entire life, I have maybe seen him 365 days in total…and not at the same time." Truth is, I should have been considered a statistic with so much going against me. I am an African-American woman who was raised by a single mother. My mother gave birth to me when she was 20, and at the time had no post high school education. My father was incarcerated before I was born, and has been for majority of my life, so my mother raised three girls pretty much alone. My father, before initially being incarcerated was both a drug dealer, and a drug abuser. He was also

Introduction: My Truth

involved in other criminal activity such as assault and armed robbery. My life was rough before I even really got a chance to live it, and to those on the outside looking in, I was doomed to fail.

Growing up, I had low self-esteem, primarily because I did not have my father in my life to tell me I was beautiful. There was no strong male figure around to tell me how I should feel about myself, show me what love was, or even be there for me when I needed to talk about "boy stuff". I didn't think I was beautiful because I had a specific definition of beauty in my mind, one fed to me by my peers, media, and my own insecurities. At the time I didn't realize how my standards of beauty became what they were, but I knew I didn't meet those standards. I said that my mother raised us pretty much alone because she married my two sisters' father, and while I loved him and respected him, I never viewed him as a father or even a father figure. I always called him by his first name and that is how I viewed him. In my opinion, there are certain roles a man has when it comes to taking care of his home and his family, and my mother filled all of those roles. She mowed the lawn, she took out the trash, she worked on her car…she did it all, and I am forever grateful for that. However, a woman should not have to teach her child everything. It takes two to make a child, and it takes two to properly raise a child. Please don't take this as a discredit to those who are single parents, as I am a huge fan and I was raised by a great one. This is simply to say that there should be two.

Growing up, we struggled financially, which did not help me to feel better about myself. Kids that I grew up around seemed to have it all, and I was wearing their hand-me-downs—little did they know. Because my mother was a single parent and worked to take care of her children, I was asked to help out with my sisters. This was something that I actually did not mind because I saw my mother being responsible and I wanted to emulate that. I remember being very young and thinking about a job, money, and my own apartment. I even thought I wanted to be emancipated because all I knew is it guaranteed my

Introduction: My Truth

own money and a place. I was so determined at such a young age, but I didn't know how much not having my father there physically was affecting my life.

When I was around the ages of seven to eleven, my father would write me from prison, and quite often. He would send me $25 here and there for Christmas and birthdays, and initially I was super excited to see those letters in the mailbox when I got home from school. At that time, in my mind, I was a "Daddy's Girl" even though my father was not physically there. I loved and adored him so much, a man that had abandoned me and my two siblings that he fathered with other women. A man that I anticipated his parole date every time it came around. Those thoughts of my father changed over time, and the older I got, the more questions I had. While his letters were still coming frequently, I was responding less and less. He began to blame my lack of response on my mother, and he assumed that she was shaming him when all the while she was encouraging me to continue communication. My discontinued communication was from the questions that I had, that I could not seem to answer: Was I not good enough for him to stay home? Did he really love me? Would any man really love me? Was he a Daddy or a Father?

These questions consumed me and at a young age I developed an analytical mindset, in which led me to believing I had an answer to everything. In my world, the answers to those questions were all "No," and that was when I realized I was not a "Daddy's Girl," but a Fatherless Daughter.

In junior high and high school, being a Fatherless Daughter was somewhat tough. I started playing sports and liking boys, and I did not have male support in either of those parts of my life. This is also the time in life when you begin to build relationships/friendships. Not having a father had a tremendous effect on how I looked at relationships and friendships, and how I conducted myself in those relationships and friendships. I dealt with abandonment issues, which is an insecurity that caused me to push people away. I tried to harm myself for

Introduction: My Truth

attention. I acted very nonchalant, which caused me to not have any life-long friendships. In my relationships, I did not practice being a "woman" because I truly did not know how to be one. I was too busy being dominant, believing that behavior was going to earn me respect and protect me from a broken heart. I did not know how to love, and did not understand love languages or what mine were. The aforementioned questions about my father would resonate in my head often and caused animosity in my spirit. I was known as the "Mean Girl" throughout my junior high and high school years and this is when I began to act out by fighting, skipping school, and seeking out other negative outlets for my inner turmoil. I was the girl who hung out with all the boys, and so I developed a false reputation of being the girl that was sleeping with the boys. The truth is, because I did not have a male figure in my life, I was seeking in them what I didn't get from him (my father).

The older I became, the more resentful I grew, and the more frustrated I became with my father. One thing that

I determined early on is I would be successful. I would not allow not having a father, and having to overcome many trials and tribulations to defeat me. The problem was, my definition of success was only to be financially stable. I did not consider being spiritually, mentally, physically, and emotionally stable a part of being successful.

As I grew older, I took steps to rectify the issues that stemmed from my lack of a father by seeking professional counseling and anger management classes. I also began to slowly communicate with my father. I wanted to correct something that was not necessarily wrong, but it just needed to be dealt with and understood. Counseling was a great asset to my life, but prayer was the best asset. My developing of my relationship with God is what has prompted me to reach my success and move into my purpose. While I did not have a father in the physical, I had and have always had One in the spiritual.

I am now twenty-something (almost 30) years old with both a Bachelor's and a Master's degree in Business

Administration. I am currently pursuing my PhD in Industrial and Organizational Psychology focusing on Coaching and Leadership. I have a Service Leadership nonprofit organization called E.L.I.T.E. Women which was established in June, 2013. The pillars of the organization are community, collaboration, mentoring, and service. The mission of E.L.I.T.E. Women is as follows:

To Encourage women to be God-fearing Leaders who Influence others to live Triumphant lifestyles, while Empowering those around them to be their best self.

I also am a member of a few other organizations, and I have been called a Servant Leader, as my leadership style is to serve others. I act as a volunteer and a host to several community events per year. I am a feminist, as I love women and what we stand for; I am a speaker; I am a daughter; I am a sister; I am a friend. I now know that I am what I say I am because God gives me the courage to believe in me.

One of my primary motivations behind this book are the girls we mentor with E.L.I.T.E. Women and the many adult conversations I've had on this topic. About 90% of the girls that we've mentored are *Fatherless Daughters*, and they suffer from many insecurities because of it. I want these young girls to know that not having a father is not the end all. There is still hope, love, strength, and a host of other qualities that can be developed without a father. I hope that my truth has been enlightening to you and encourages you to reach new levels of understanding and strength. In this book, you will hear from me and other successful women who are fatherless, but learned to not allow what they lack to affect what they stand to gain.

Being a Single Mother is Usually not a Choice

I know I mentioned this somewhat previously, but I felt a need to address this more directly and personally. As I prepare for this book, as I write this book, and as I discuss fatherlessness with other women, I realize that there could be a misperception that being a single mother is a bad thing. I am here to tell you that in my opinion it is not, however it is usually not a choice that a woman makes.

In reality, there are some things that a child learns from a woman, their mother, and there are also things that a child should get from their father. Without a father, or even without a mother, a child naturally adapts to their circumstances and are forced to learn certain things on their own. With this can come trauma, trials, heartbreaks, and disappointments and had you have a nuclear household, some things may have been avoided. This is not to say that that you will not have trauma, trials, disappointments, and heartbreaks if you have both parents actively in your life, but there would definitely be a difference in how those things are handled.

Let's take a look at it from this perspective. When you are raised by a single-mother, you naturally adopt a lot of your mother's characteristics, morals, and values. If you see your mother doing something, you either grow up to believe that it is the right thing to do, or the total opposite. If you only have one perspective, it is likely that you may follow that one perspective and possibly bump your head a few times before you get things right. On the other hand, if you have both parents actively in your life, you have more perspectives to choose from. You are more likely to make better choices in some situations because you have two people telling you the same things as opposed to one.

I felt a strong need to just to add my personal opinion on this topic, because I was raised by a single mother and she did the best that she could with what she had. She made sure that me and my two sisters had what we needed and for that I am forever grateful. While I am proud of the woman I have become and had my circumstance been different, I may not be the person I am today, I recognize the struggle that my mother had to face. I have seen my mother cry because she had to do it alone, and I know that it wasn't her choice to have to do it that way. My mother recognized God as her Savior and she is fully aware of Him being the reason why we all are here, but not have the man who helped make me be there to assist in raising me was difficult at times. With that said, a single mother is a strong, sometimes unconsciously driven, constantly encouraged, and God-Fearing Queen in my eyes. There is so much beauty in women and especially in a woman who develops strength from her circumstances. She didn't ask to do alone, but she did, and she did it with all that she had. Was it a choice? No. Is it ever a choice? Rarely. But she did it, and for that, every woman who is a part of this project, regardless to her perspective, is appreciative of the woman who at times, had to do it alone, even though it was not her choice.

Chapter One

Understand The Curse... Break The Curse!

It is said that children who are fatherless are more likely to live in poverty, use drugs, suffer from health and emotional problems, and drop out of school. These are curses that one, especially a child, can easily fall into if one's thoughts of being fatherless are allowed to become more powerful than thoughts of living out their purpose.

Something that is important for everyone to understand, especially women like us (Fatherless Daughters), is the definition of a generational curse. A generational curse is the inheritance of misfortunes. An example is a father who beats his wife, and their children grow up and become abusive. A generational curse is not necessarily something that is seen, but is most likely something that is unseen. By that I mean, while you may see something going on in your household, you may not see yourself doing the exact same thing. There are many traits that I inherited from a man that I did not see, my father. For example, my father is a very impulsive and reactionary person, and before understanding this about him and myself, I was the exact same way. What's crazy to me is my mother had three girls and we were all raised in the same household. We all have traits from my mother, but there was always something different about me, and I did not grasp why until I was almost an adult.

The earlier you are able to recognize the curse in which you were born into, the sooner you are able to break it. When you begin to notice those unseen traits, you can start to change them. You recognize patterns and this is when true development and growth of self begins.

If you are living based on how your family lived before you were even born, you have not started your true growth. Now, this isn't to say that you won't have some traits of your family members, but when we go back to the definition of generational curse, and analyze the word "misfortune", we understand that any trait that brings you misfortune can and must be changed. I have prepared four steps that will assist you in breaking generational curses:

1. **Recognize and Surrender**

   You first have to recognize it. Recognizing requires true self-reflection. Once you recognize the generational curse, you have to surrender it to God. You have to allow Him to lead your life in the way that it should go. You have to understand that while things may not have played out the way that you think it should have, it has played out the way that God allowed it. You have to be conscious of when behaviors of generational curses appear and know how to deactivate them. Your test is your testimony and someone else's blessing.

2. Be Willing to Forgive

Once you have recognized and surrendered all negativity to God, you have to fully commit to forgiveness. It is easy to hold on to grudges, guilt, anger, and hate, but it can be extremely difficult to truly forgive. I will go more into forgiving others in the next chapter, but here I'd like to express the importance of forgiving yourself. It is often said that in order to forgive someone, you must first forgive yourself, and this is the absolute truth. We have to forgive ourselves for holding grudges, hate, and anger. As a Fatherless Daughter, it is very much possible for you to fall in some of the statistics of being fatherless. You may have indulged in drugs, sex, and or alcohol. You may have suffered from emotional insecurities. You may have even suffered from the Fatherless Daughter Syndrome, which is an emotional disorder that leads to repeated dysfunctional relationships. Even if you are currently dealing with some of these issues, recognizing it is half the battle. Now it is about correcting it and forgiving yourself for it.

Most of us began to identity with fatherlessness as children. This means that as we became adults, we still held onto some of those childlike ways subconsciously. For example, as a child who is fatherless, you may be quick to walk away from a friendship because that person did not do what you wanted them to do. This is childlike and it needs to be addressed. Now that you know, grow up so that you can GO UP. Once you forgive yourself, the healing process begins and you can forgive those who you feel have wronged you.

3. **Break the Curse**

Now that you have recognized and surrendered, and forgiven yourself and the person(s) you feel have wronged you, you are now able to break the curse. You now have the ability to change the way you think. Once you change the way you think, your actions and behaviors begin to change. You are breaking the cycle! You are breaking every chain, every curse that has held you back. The best part about this is you are establishing a new future for those who will come after you, like your children.

4. **Manifest it with your Mouth**

Speak aloud that you are going to break every chain and every curse, and speak it in the mighty name of Jesus. The tongue is powerful, and is the beginning of everything that happens in your life. If you say it and believe it, it is so! Amen! This goes for the good and the bad. Just as speaking positively can affect great positive change in your life, speaking words of doubt or negativity can slow down the change you want, so watch what comes out of your mouth and even what goes through your mind. Practicing these four steps will lead you to a better place in your life and straighten your path. These steps will help you to recognize how God intended you to live and how He's perfected you. Psalms 139:14 states, **"I praise you because I am fearfully and wonderfully made; your works are wonderful, I know that well."** This verse uses nothing but positivity to describe how we are made, and that God wants us to live out a wonderful life. A curse is not wonderful, but the complete opposite. Now that you are aware that you could possibly not be living the way that God intended, do something about it! Be intentional with your mind, be intentional with your heart, and be intentional with your actions. Learn to be present and focus on what is in front of you and not behind you.

Lamentations 5:7 (NIV) states, **"Our ancestors sinned and are no more, and we bear their punishment"**

When I read this verse, my interpretation is, "my family's sin is my sin." I found out some years ago that my father did not meet his mother until he was eight years old and he has seen his father a total of five times in his entire life. My father, while upset that he did not find out who his mother was sooner, grew to love his mother, but despised his father. He suffered from depression, low self-esteem, and a host of other things primarily due to not having a male figure in his life. This also led to drugs and his imprisonment, not only physically, but mentally. As he began to age, he found himself repeating what happened to him in the lives of his own children. He was an absent father, and when he was younger, he felt that being absent was the best for his children. He did not realize at the time that he was perpetuating a generational curse. Had he understood the true impact of his father being absent in his life, it would have helped him to better understand the impact of him being absent in his children's lives. While I had been discovering and utilizing coping mechanisms in high school, I still was upset, but I was fatherless and had to deal with it. Knowing this information about my father helped me to develop an understanding of him. Understanding him in turn aided in me understanding myself and allowed me to open my heart to breaking generational curses that were long overdue. Once my understanding was firm and clear, I was able to truly forgive and begin to cultivate a nurturing relationship with my father. While we still have some ways to go, we have come far. God has softened my heart and made me a person of love, and for that I am forever grateful.

Chapter Two

Love And Forgiveness

Love

I first want to talk about love, and I'm talking about the real, true love because in order to forgive, you must first know love. As Fatherless Daughters, we sometimes do not develop a true understanding of love (outside of family love) until we experience a few heartbreaks with a man. The reason for this is because when you do not have a father or father figure, the first way we usually learn to love a male is seeking it from men through dating. While the love for a mate and the love for a father is different, they are also very similar. Most of us have heard women say that they look for in a man what they have in their father. Well that is how the two relate. When you grow to build a loving relationship with a man, you want him to be an umbrella; you want a man that will protect you from the rain but still be close by when the sun is shining, as it could start raining at any time. As children, we desire that same exact thing from a father; love and protection. When you don't have a father, or at least a strong male figure, that is a part of love that may take you a little longer to discover,

I am sure that some of you are familiar with this verse, but the Bible states that Love is the following:

"Love is patient and kind. Love is not jealous, it does not brag, and it is not proud. Love is not rude, is not selfish, and does not get upset with others. Love does not count up wrongs that have been done. Love takes no pleasure in evil, but rejoices over the truth. Love patiently accepts all things. It always trust, always hopes, and always endures. Love never ends. There are

gifts of prophecy, but they will always be ended. There are gifts of speaking in different languages, but those gifts will stop. There is a gift of knowledge, but it will come to an end." 1 Corinthians 13:4-8 (NCV)

I have always been a fan of this verse, even as a child, and at that time, I did not understand what true love was. It was just so beautifully and poetically written, and I knew that this is what love was supposed to be. We naturally learn to "love" our parents and our family, but when we start to recognize, realize, and experience certain things in life, our definition of love begins to change. It is important to understand that love can never turn into hate, and if it has, it was never love in the first place. Know that!

Just like with forgiveness, in order to love others, we must first learn to love ourselves. Self-love often takes time because as we grow, we sometimes learn to love a fabricated self. By that, I mean we love the person with make-up, whose hair is fly, who has a good job, a degree, a nice car, and a nice home. Do you love yourself when you are stripped of all of those materialistic things? Do you love yourself when you are broke and have been broken? You need to learn to love yourself bare. Sometimes this does not happen until you are stripped of everything. Understand that the breaking is only temporary and builds character. Below are some steps that you can take to truly learn to love yourself.

1. **Understand your pain and take responsibility for your feelings.**

    Understanding your pain and taking responsibility for your feelings means just that. Own it! When you understand the things or people that cause you anguish, and you are able to truly see the source of that pain, the healing from that pain can begin. This is the beginning to loving you. For example, being a Fatherless Daughter, you have to admit that there is some pain that was derived from that. You have to understand this pain and learn to cope with it. Figure out what works for you. For me, I like to journal, I love poetry, and I enjoy reading encouraging books. That is how I cope. Once you have understood your pain, take responsibility for and own your feelings. Your feelings, even if they are negative, are yours and you have every right to have them, and no one can take them away from you.

2. **Take the time to really learn just who you are.**

In order to love you, you have to know you… BARE. Strip yourself of everything and figure out who you are. Praying, reading, meditating, centering your thoughts, and being present are ways you can learn who you are. Take a specific time of each day to focus on you. Focus on your wants, needs, and desires. Make sure your wants, needs, and desires are spiritually aligned and your love for yourself will begin to ooze. Trust me!

3. **Do not be afraid to be who you are.**

Sometimes when you are a little more unique, or a little quirkier, you want to hide those things. YOU SHOULD NOT. Be you and do you because NO ONE can do it better. Understand that it is okay to want to change and develop yourself, as that is the way to life, but in the meantime, still remain true to who you are. Love you.

4. **Care about yourself just as much as you care about others.**

This is sometimes difficult. When you are a person of love, you care about and love on people so much that you may sometimes forget to care for and love on yourself. Make sure that your health is in order. Make sure that you are spiritually and mentally sound. Take care of your physical outer appearance. You do not want to look like what you have been through. Some will say that this is being selfish, but you can't give your best self if you aren't your best self. Best self requires self-care.

Forgiveness

Forgiveness is something that comes from the heart and comes from love. Some of us are Fatherless because our father made a choice, while some of us are Fatherless because our fathers are deceased. Whatever the reason may be, what most of us have or have had in common is that we have not forgiven our fathers for their choices or lack thereof. When you haven't forgiven, you have to evaluate the way that you love and whether or not it is real love. It is also important to understand that forgiving does not necessarily mean that you have to be active in your father's life. The Bible states to honor your Mother and Father, as your days will be longer[2]. Depending on the situation, sometimes honoring may mean keeping your distance. Forgiveness is an essential aspect of truly learning yourself and also developing yourself. A lack of forgiveness can hinder you and cause many issues in your current and future relationships. While I am sure that you have heard this before, many people do not grasp this until it is too late. I can honestly say that I have forgiven my father. I love him, and I love him unconditionally. I have realized that our situation sometimes requires separation as there is some personal

---

[2] Exodus 20:12

development that needs to take place on both ends and some things cannot be worked through together.

Once you love yourself, you can truly learn to love others properly and forgive. This is when true understanding of the previously mentioned scripture takes place. Love is patient, which means that things won't happen when you want, how you want, and where you want, but your love for someone will remain the same regardless. True love is unconditional, which means it is absolute. It will not be predicated upon if someone makes you upset or doesn't do or buy you what you want. When you become a person of love, you attract love and it becomes easy for you to love honestly, which also makes it easier for you to forgive.

Below, I want you to do an exercise that will help you to forgive and also help you understand the power of forgiveness (If you need additional space, please refer to the notes section located in the back of this book).

1. Write about something you wish to forgive someone for (Not necessarily your father).

_____
_____
_____
_____
_____
_____
_____

2. Think about ways you can take responsibility for your actions.

_____
_____
_____
_____
_____
_____
_____

3. Think of reasons for which you may need to seek forgiveness.

_____
_____
_____
_____
_____
_____
_____

4. Forgiving someone begins in your heart and mind. How do you plan to forgive them personally?

_____
_____
_____
_____
_____

5. Write down the names of those you need to forgive and repeat exercise.

_____

_____

_____

_____

_____

_____

_____

_____

I will always end exercises with either you personally praying or me praying. I will do it this time, but next time it is on you.

*Dear Heavenly **Father**,*

We have come to You thanking You for all things. For You are the giver of life and for that we appreciate You forever. Father, we ask that You first massage our hearts so that they are easier to open. Open our hearts to forgiveness and love. Help us to love ourselves and others like You love us. Help us to also forgive ourselves and others like You have and continue to forgive us. Give us wisdom, pour into us love, and bless us in our journey moving forward.

In *Jesus* name, we pray,

Amen.

Chapter Three

Your Past Does Not Determine Your Future

It really doesn't! As women, we tend to be emotional, and we allow our emotions to dictate our mood. This is something that we have in common with our younger selves; we allowed our emotions to dictate our mood and our behaviors. Growing up without one of your parents, especially a father, can lead to many different behaviors such as anger, promiscuity, and lack of self-respect. It is important to recognize those behaviors early on so that you are able to understand them and control them. This chapter will provide ways for you to not allow your past to determine your future.

Stop throwing yourself a pity party! Stop talking and thinking about what you don't have now, what you didn't have growing up, and comparing yourself to others. Realize that you have your own path to walk and as long as you stay on that path, you will be exactly where you should be at all times. It is when we start worrying about the path that someone else is on and comparing it's smoothness to ours, we end up veering off of our own path and getting lost. I was guilty of this for many years, and even drove myself to depression because of it. It seemed like everyone around me was doing much better than I was, whether it be financially, spiritually, or mentally. I was so focused on other people and their success that I was not focusing on me and what my success looked like. I had to realize that my behavior and thought processes were not aiding in my future success, and they were not in line with the law of attraction. First, let me say that I am a strong believer in the law of attraction and manifestation. The law of attraction simply states that whatever you think about are what will manifest. With that said, it is important to focus on what it is that you want for your life. It is also important to understand that there is a difference between focusing on what you want in your life and focusing on what is wrong in your life. For example, when you think about that new car that you want, you believe that you will have that new car, you know that you have the car before it is actually in your possession, you actually imagine yourself sitting in the driver's seat and driving the car. My car is an Audi A7, fully loaded, and I have it! I'm actually sitting in it right now (wink, wink…manifestation). With constant vision, faith, and work, you will have that car. You will attract it. On the contrary, if your focus is currently on that old car that you have and have put money into, but it still isn't running, then you are attracting negative thoughts and not that new car. In order to ensure that your past does not dictate your future, you want to gain control of your thoughts first and understand the law of attraction.

Before turning to the next page, I want you to take a moment and think about your past. Now think about your current situation. Is there anything about you, such as attitude, current career, or disposition that you think are derived from your past? Has this attitude, current career selection, or disposition attributed to your success? On the next page, I ask that you use the space provided to evaluate your past and how it has influenced your present, both negatively and positively. This exercise is meant for you to reflect on your past and be honest with yourself. I want you to see how the past has affected you so it doesn't continue to do so.

Evaluate Your Past

Your Past Does Not Determine Your Future

Now that you have revisited the past and evaluated the present, it should be easier to ensure that, from this day forth, your future is successful.

After evaluating the past and looking at the present, you now want to practice being conscious. By this, I mean making sure you don't slip back into old habits. You want to stay aware and in control of your actions. For example, if it has been a part of your daily routine to use profanity and you are wanting to stop, it is important to be aware of every time it seems to almost slip out of your mouth so that you catch yourself. Instead of saying the actual bad word, replace the word with a filler words or create a swear jar. Remain aware of your old habits, and remember that any habit can be broken.

So we have looked into our past and our present to determine how to ensure that we have a successful future, and we have also learned what it is to be conscious, I want us to take a look at our younger selves one more time. Some years ago, I wrote a letter to my younger self. When I wrote this letter, it took me back to a time where there was once darkness. It took me about an hour to write this letter, and there was joy and pain that came from writing it. It helped me to see the transitions that I had made in my life and helped me to understand the potential that I have. It showed me a lot about my strengths, my character, and my faith. I know that this may seem like a lot of writing for the third chapter, but I want you to take a moment to think about this. What would you tell that person? How would you encourage that person? How is she different from the person you are today? Was that person hurt and in denial? Did she experience things that she never discussed with anyone? Was she angry, and did some of her actions show it? Really think about her, and on the next page, write a "Dear Self" letter. Focus on your test and testimonies, and realize that your mess can be someone else's message. Once you have completed your letter, you should remove the pages, place them in a place that is dear to you, somewhere where you can always look back at it. This letter is a way to keep you conscious of who you were, who you are, and who you are to become.

Fatherless Daughter: A Different Perspective

Dear _____,

Your Past Does Not Determine Your Future

Please take a brief moment to pray now that you have written your "Dear Self" letter. Thank God for your trials and tribulations, and also thank Him for His grace and mercy. Remember that your trials made you into the remarkable woman you are today and it only gets better from here.

How did writing the letter make you feel? Do you feel relieved? Like you have had a weight lifted off of your shoulder? You should, because these are the first steps of you taking control of your life and ensuring that your future is successful. I hope that this chapter has given you hope and has kept you engaged. In the next chapter, we will discuss prioritization and setting measurable goals.

Chapter Four

Prioritize Your Life, Set Goals, And Start Early!

It is important to understand that your life is YOUR life and it is up to you to prioritize, goal-set, and start as early as you can. If you have not started before reading this book, then make it a priority to start NOW.

Being women without fathers, it is safe to say that we may not have had much "structure" in our life growing up. We often are not taught early on by our parent how to prioritize, but we may sometimes see our parent's structure and adopt it. I personally come from a parent who grew up in a household with both parents, but their household was not structured. Because of that and my mother being a single parent of three girls, we weren't provided structure either. That is not to say that my mother wasn't the best mother, as she did the best that she could and she made sure that we were young God-fearing ladies that respected ourselves. But because she was the only person responsible for us, she spent more time at work and financially providing, and less time emotionally developing and providing structure.

This book is intended for you to learn to cope and grow, but it is also an interactive tool. Reading words on a page can help some, but being involved will help most. Prioritizing your life requires you to put your priorities on paper. I recommend purchasing a daily planner and a journal, and making a conscious effort to write in them daily. I have a planner that has a word of encouragement for each day, and it helps me to start every day on the right foot. I also have a daily journal that I write in. Both of these tools help me to self-reflect and improve. I know some of you may be reading this and thinking, "What about using a planner/calendar on my phone or the Notes application on my phone?" While those are options, there is something much more powerful about physically writing out your priorities and goals, and referencing them often. I believe that there is manifestation in your ink once it is on paper.

On the next page, there is an activity that is intended to assist in prioritization. Prioritizing is arranging things in order of importance. Before you arrange your life in order of importance, you have to first realize what is important to you. It is important that you take advantage of the interactive tools that this book provides, as it has been proven to help women who are Fatherless Daughters to overcome obstacles that they may or may not have realized that they have been dealing with.

1. Think about the most important things in your life and anything that may become important within the next six months. Write them out.

Prioritize Your Life, Set Goals, And Start Early!

_____
_____
_____
_____
_____
_____
_____
_____
_____
_____
_____
_____
_____
_____

2. Make a list of the things that you spend a lot of time thinking about, and what you find yourself doing a lot of.

_____
_____

_____

_____

_____

_____

_____

_____

_____

_____

_____

_____

_____

Now it is time to goal set. On this page, based on what you wrote on the previous page, write out your goals for the next twelve months. Now, if you want to set quarterly goals, you can, but I recommend goal setting for an entire year. The space provided is intended for you to set goals for every three months. If you want to set goals for every month, you can continue your list in the notes section at the tail end of the book.

Month: _____

_____
_____
_____
_____
_____
_____
_____
_____

Month: _____

_____
_____
_____
_____
_____

_____
_____
_____
_____

Month: _____

_____
_____
_____
_____
_____
_____
_____
_____

Month: _____

_____
_____

_____

_____

_____

_____

_____

_____

_____

Now what I want you to do is transfer your first set of goals to an index card. Take the index card and place it somewhere that you constantly look, like your purse, wallet, desk at work, nightstand, etc. Pay attention to when the three months past and how you have reached your goals. The reason is because you will self-consciously program yourself to visualize your goals because you see them every day.

"Intention without action is an insult to those who expect the best from you."

~Andy Andrews

Chapter Five

Create A Vision And Edit As You Go

C hapter four encouraged you to prioritize and goal set, and we also talked a little about vision. I will now discuss creating a vision, editing as you go, and manifesting that vision. As Fatherless Daughters, it becomes difficult sometimes to see the light at the end of the tunnel. You sometimes focus on the negatives and what you don't have, rather than focusing on what you do have and the ability you have to create a vision for yourself.

Vision is defined as the faculty or state of being able to see. A visionary is one who thinks about or plans their future with imagination, creativity, and wisdom. A true visionary usually maps out a plan, something like a business plan, but for their life. We all have developed an imagination and grown wiser from previous situations and circumstances, and it is now time to determine how to put these things to good use. As stated in the previous chapter, it is good to set short-term goals and work your way up to long-term goals. An exercise that I practice regularly is to write 1-3 goals on an index card, and place a deadline on those goals, but the deadline is within three months' time of me writing them. I write the three-month deadline on the index card, and I give each goal a more specific timeframe. Once I have written these goals, I place sticky notes in areas I look at often, like the refrigerator, bathroom mirror, headboard, etc., so that I am reminded of my goals daily. This helps me to create a vision, and after seeing my goals in different places, I begin to literally see my goals being accomplished. Now between setting the goal and the goal deadline, there is one step that is crucial to the success of completing your goals, and that is to map out a plan of how to complete the goals. For example, if a goal of yours is to pay off a bill within the next three months, the first thing you want to do is create a budget for paying off that bill. You have to know and understand how your money is being allocated. Once you have a budget, you can now determine how much you can afford to put away to go towards your goal. I would also recommend that you put away a little extra if at all possible. Doing this helps you to physically see that your goals can be accomplished. This may or may not be an easy thing to do, but it can be done.

When goal setting, you should seek out an accountability partner. This person will be there to remind you of your goals, talk to you through accomplishing your goals, and encourage you when you are struggling. Remember that goal setting isn't always easy, but it is always worth it. The feeling of accomplishment is comparable to nothing else in this world, and when you have someone to share your accomplishments with, it is even better.

How We Go Wrong

1. *Discouragement*

    One way a person can go wrong is when he or she begins to goal set, and does not accomplish that goal by a specific timeframe, he or she becomes discouraged and stops. That person stops visualizing positivity for themselves and they just give up. This is one of the main reasons an accountability partner is so crucial. Know that you can edit your goals and deadlines, but it is not something that you want to make a habit out of. Try to stay on track as much as possible. Truth is, things may come up that may throw you off of your initial plan. Don't fret. The enemy never wants you to win, and he will always be there attempting to deter you. Be diligent and understand that there is no one stronger than someone with a vision other than the one who has a vision and a spirit of execution.

2. *Fear of Success or Failure*

    There are many people with a fear of failure, but there are equally, if not more people who have a fear of success.

This is actually an issue I suffered from. Some people focus on the negative and think that with success comes hate, and that scares some people away from goal setting. Then you have the people who have a fear of failure, and because of that negative thinking, the law of attraction is ignited (as discussed in a previous chapter), and failure will come to you. You will succeed because of you, but you can also fail because of you. Set a clear vision of success in your head, and go for it.

3. *If You Fail to Plan, You Plan to Fail*

This old adage is very true. As stated previously, when you set a goal, you want to make sure that you have a plan to succeed. It is easy to write out a goal on a piece of paper, but the planning process can be a little tricky. That is why you want to focus on a plan. I always say, "Write it out!" When you see something on paper, it becomes easier to accomplish because you can visualize it. Although this isn't my preference, another way to plan is to use the technology that you use on a day to day basis: your cellphone. There are hundreds of applications that you can download that can assist in the planning process depending on what your goal is. Maximize all of your resources. While these are only a few ways that one can go wrong, it is imperative to be Positive and have a Plan. These two P's alone can lead you to the path of success. Being a Fatherless Daughter definitely can be a struggle, but the moment you realize that there is a blessing in your circumstance, you begin to live your true life. I have given you my truth and my methods, and hopefully by this point you have found out some truths about yourself. Several chapters after this one will provide you with stories of women who have been without a father and their perspective. They will also share their trials, coping mechanisms and how they were able to pursue their dreams and be successful despite. The hope is that everyone reading this book will be able to relate in some way to every one of these women's testimonies.

Chapter Six

Unveiling The Truth After Death

There is more than one way that a young girl can end up fatherless, and as for the young woman whose perspective is portrayed in this chapter, it is death. She named her chapter, "Unveiling the Truth after Death" because of her truths that she discovered after her father passed.

Nicole was just 11 years old when she was picked up by her mother from school on a Friday, which was odd because her dad usually picked her up. When she got home, her mother said to her, "I got some news to tell you". Due to being filled with emotion, Nicole's mother ran into the bathroom, and Nicole followed asking what was wrong. This is the day that Nicole found out her father had been murdered.

Nicole's dad was involved in selling drugs, and one of his customers was his boss. Despite Nicole's dad's choice to sell drugs, which was what he looked at as a way to take care of his family, he was a great dad in Nicole's eyes.

On the Friday of his murder, his boss did not show up to work and it was payday. Him and a few of his co-workers decided to go to his bosses home to find out what was going on and hopefully pick up their paychecks. When they got to their boss's home, Nicole's dad was the one who went in to talk to him. When he went in, his boss began to ask him about the drugs and Nicole's dad informed him that he did not have any drugs on him. The boss became irate and repeatedly demanded the drugs, which turned into confrontation. As Nicole's dad and his boss argued about paychecks and drugs, the boss pulled out a gun and shot Nicole's dad in the head, killing him.

Nicole's Perspective

Nicole's father not being present in her life was not an actual choice of his, but choosing to live the lifestyle that he did was his choice. While he may have thought that living that way was best for his family, his choices ultimately ended his life. At the time of her father's death, Nicole's mother and father were separated, and Nicole blamed her mother for the separation. This led to her partially blaming her mother for his death. She believed that if they had not separated, her father would not have felt a need to sell drugs to provide for his family. Because of these feelings, this drove a wedge between her and her mother at a young age.

Nicole's Trials

Nicole growing up without her father caused many insecurities, some which we all face being fatherless. She has dealt with trust issues, control issues, and instabilities. Some of these things weren't realized until we sat down and interviewed. Throughout our interview, I told her of some of my insecurities and not only did we realized what insecurities we shared, but she realized why she does some of the things she does or why she reacts to certain situations in the manner in which she does. For example, I shared with her that a previous insecurity of mine was abandonment issues. I thought that as a father, you are not to leave your child and because mine did, I believed that everyone would eventually leave, and sometimes I would also push people away. When I would lose friends, I would be very nonchalant about losing a friend. I really acted as if I did not care. It was truly an act. That was not who I was at the core, but only who I pretended to be to protect myself. What I thought was protecting me was harming me emotionally. Nicole was the exact same way and is admittedly still dealing with this.

Nicole's Success

While Nicole is still on her journey to being what God has called her to be, she has achieved a lot. First, Nicole has matured and has taken a path of forgiveness; forgiveness of her mom, forgiveness of her father, and most importantly, forgiveness of herself. She clung to guilt and anger after her father's death, and she has since sought out healing from her spiritual Father.

She is currently the General Manager for a Christian Bookstore which has been nothing short of a blessing to her life. Being in that position, she has not only changed her life, but she has been a blessing to many, and many have been a blessing to her. She has prayed over people, she has spoken at conferences, and she is an ordained minister, speaking every fifth Sunday at her church. Her calendar continues to fill with events that are the Lords work, and she is truly flowing in her gifts.

Her story inspires us all because you may have lost your physical father, but your spiritual father is still taking care of you and guiding you into your purpose. Even through the tough times, listen to Him and allow Him to carry you through.

Author's Perspective

With this book project, I wanted to it to be clear that everyone does not have everything figured out. To be in a situation such as fatherlessness, there is always room to grow and to learn. It is important to understand that everyone's journey is different. What may be easy for you may be difficult for others. Some women do not realize immediately why they are the way that they are, or why they respond in the way that they respond, and it may take a little longer for one to discover this. Once you discover that there are some traits and possibly some dysfunctions that have developed because you do not have your father, you able to combat it. In Nicole's case, there are some things that had not been considered until she was interviewed for this project. Now that she is aware, she can begin to address the issues and move forward. This will lead to even greater success in the future.

Chapter Seven

The Good, The Bad, And The Ugly

When discussing fatherlessness, the bad and the ugly are usually what the topic surrounds, but rarely do we discuss the potential good that can come from being fatherless or growing up without a parent. What is sad is that it is typical to place children in categories when they are fatherless at a young age. You never hear anyone say, "Because she is fatherless, she is going to be a fighter and be successful." You usually hear, "She doesn't have a father, and that is why she is behaving that way." I am here to tell you that while there may be a lot of bad and ugly, and if allowed it will consume you, there can also be good. It just may be a little more difficult to find at first. Let's take a look at some positive traits that women acquire from being fatherless.

Go Getter

From my preparing to write this book, interviews, and conversations, every Fatherless Daughter I have encountered is a "Go Getter," and her not having a father contributed to this. When you grow up fatherless, you sometimes grow up with the mentality that you are not enough. Now, while this isn't a good feeling to have or live with, it usually manifests into a go-getter mentality. Your focus begins to shift from you not being enough to proving that you are more than enough. Every woman who is a part of this project is successful, and they are successful because they are all go-getters. They all goal set, they plan, and they are sure to achieve their goals. Whether they realize it or not, they all follow the law of attraction and it starts when they shift their thoughts from a negative to a positive. You too can do this if you haven't learned this powerful tool already. If you change the way that you think, you are truly able to tap into power within that allows you to change your life.

Prepared for Life's Trials

Being fatherless or identifying with being fatherless prepares you for life's trials. Whether you are fatherless because your father passed or because your father did not desire to be present in your life, there is a sadness that is shared. When you heal from the sadness and grasp an understanding of how every situation prepares you for the next, it gives you a strength that you did not have before. This strength prepares you for most of life's trials and tribulations. The hurt of not having the first man tell you that you are beautiful be your father defines a new truth for you. This truth leads to a readiness for what is next. Be careful to not allow this to influence a pessimistic way of thinking. You can easily divert to thinking that, "everything bad happens to me" instead of seeing this as a blessing of power and preparedness.

Develop a Stronger Relationship with Your Spiritual Father

When you are fatherless, you sometimes try to find the love you are missing from your father in others. Sometimes it is in your mother, sometimes it is in friends, and a lot of times it is in a man. Most of us has been through this. The key is to go to the right man. The only Man that can fill a void is our Father in Heaven. His words says that He will never leave us or forsake us[3]. The moment we take those words seriously is the moment we start to realize that it was our Father who was protecting us from harm's way. When we hone in on the fact that it was Him keeping us the entire time, it increases our desire to want to know Him. We question, "Who is this Man that loves us unconditionally? No matter what I do, He loves me the same. I have to get to know Him." Yes, there is bad and ugly to being fatherless, but there can also be good, bad, and ugly to coming from a two-parent household. Adapting and adjusting to your situation helps in seeing the strength that can come from this.

---

[3] Deuteronomy 31:6

Chapter Eight

Kind Of Like A Nice Uncle

As Brandi and I sat in the comfort of her home on a very warm June day, we discussed the impact of her parents' divorce on her life, how she once identified herself as a Fatherless Daughter and her perspective on fatherlessness.

"Kind of Like a Nice Uncle" was developed because after Brandi's parents divorced, that is how she viewed her father: an uncle is a loved one who may show up for life celebrations (some birthdays or maybe a graduation) but doesn't fill the role of a father. At the age of 27, Brandi can remember back to the tender age of three when her parents were arguing and yelling. This was odd to her because that was not the type of household she grew up in, and once the argument ended, her father walked out the door, never to return to their home. To see a father walk out of the home at such a young age and remember it can have a tremendous effect on not only children, but also adults. It takes a developed strength to be able to deal with and truly move on from abandonment.

Brandi experienced hate, low self-esteem, pain, and anger growing up without her father being as present as she wanted him to be. Yes, she did see him every summer, but she wanted him to be more present in her life. Once she was older, Brandi talked to both of her parents to find out why they divorced, she determined that it was due to lack of communication and issues with monogamy. That knowledge played a major role in how she has developed as a woman. Brandi and her father now have a strong relationship, and she has been very intentional in developing an understanding of him for the betterment of what is to come in their future.

Brandi's Perspective

Brandi's parents were married for about four years and they were dating for five years prior to getting married. When her parents divorced, her father moved to Atlanta, which drove a deeper wedge in their relationship. Her views on what a father is and what a father does began to change the longer he wasn't around consistently. She then began to realize that he would not be returning anytime soon. During the interview, Brandi was asked what her perspective is on a "father" and on a "daddy" and what the difference was to her. Her answer was quite different than most:

"A father to me is the role description. I think it is more than biological. Like, when I hear the word 'father', I think about the man who teaches you about the world. The man who protects you from harm. The first man to tell you that you are beautiful and worthy of love. A father is your first example in the world of what a man should be and what a man can be. That should be the standard of a man, a father. 'Daddy!' [chuckles] I would say is what most black girls have instead of a father. I think that is why baby-daddy is such a common term. I know people say daddy's girl, but it has a reverse effect in my mind. It's a lot of men walking around with the title of 'daddy', like that's my daddy, or that's my baby-daddy. There are not a lot of women or young girls who say, 'that is my father.' I actually met a little girl who has a father and refers to her dad as father and when I saw that, I was like '[expletive]', I wish I had that."

Author's Perspective

I found Brandi's definition of a father versus a daddy to be very interesting. Her perspective is one I had not considered until I was provided a clear breakdown and her understanding of the two. I always looked at a father as being the donor to create the child and the daddy as the one who is there for the child. In my eyes, daddy is more personal and signifies a strong bond, whereas father only signifies to me the Merriam-Webster definition of a father.

Brandi's Trials

Brandi came to the realization that she was fatherless at the age of three. The man who was technically her father, seemed more like a really nice uncle. As previously stated, Brandi's parents were divorced due to communication and monogamy issues. While she may not have realized it growing up, she now sees how the divorce played a major role in the way she has developed as a woman. As she puts it, she loved her dad for a long time after the divorce because her mother was great at protecting his honor, but at some point the love began to change. She started to question if she was loveable and how worthy she was of love. When she was about six or seven years old, she recalls moving to a different neighborhood. She remembers her mom telling her that her father was in another state, busy working really hard and all the planes in the world could not bring him back even though he wanted to come back. Tearfully, Brandi shared that she would make her best friend at the time, join her to chase airplanes down the street and they would yell, "dad...dad, I'm here!" At that time, she wanted so badly for her dad to come back, and while they would talk often, she realized that there was nothing that she could do to bring her father home. She often questioned herself at a very young age about what it was that she was missing or what she didn't have that would make him not want to come back to her.

This reminds me of what many of us fatherless daughters face. Many of us think that it is our fault or something that we are lacking that keeps our fathers away from us. It is usually not until we become adults that we realize that we are not responsible for the decisions that anyone makes, including fathers.

Brandi experienced fatherlessness all throughout her adolescent years because of how angry she was with her father. She recalls one particular summer when she was at her father's home in Atlanta. He was in the bedroom with one of his girlfriends. She could hear them chuckling and doing whatever adults do, and she remembers wondering when he was going to come out and give her a goodnight kiss, as this is what she was accustomed to with her mother. She stayed up for hours waiting, and when she realized that he wasn't coming out, she cried herself to sleep. She felt like her dad was there for the fun things like summer vacations, but when she cried herself to sleep at night or if a boy broke her heart, he was not there.

Brandi's Success

Brandi has experienced success in many ways, and she also defines success in many ways. The fact that she currently has a relationship with her father is a huge success to her. From her point-of-view, it shows that she has achieved a level of forgiveness that many do not. In Brandi's words, "forgiveness is a sign of a successful spirit." Her father is still in Atlanta and their newfound relationship is slowly growing over time as they are learning to trust one another. She took the time to understand him by asking questions and listening carefully. She asked him two to three years ago, what was the state of their relationship, and he replied with, "We don't have a relationship." Instead of getting upset, she worked with him to understand his definition of relationship and what she needed to do to be a better daughter. They have grown to a place where they have a blossoming relationship and communicate frequently.

Brandi further elaborates on what it took for her to forgive, stating that what was most important in her steps to forgiveness was experiencing adulthood for herself. She thought about her parent's age at the time of their marriage. She spoke to both parents about their romantic life and their requirements in a romantic relationship. The quote she lives by in this situation is, "Giving up the chance for a better past." Giving up the chance for her three-year-old self to have the father that she wanted in order to embrace the father she currently has. She had to change her definition of a father so she could to accept him as a father. She had to forgive herself and understand that he is and has always been human; which means he makes mistakes. She had to understand some of the generational adversity that both parents have experienced. She does not condone his infidelity, but she accepts it. She had to understand that the type of daughter she was being in her adolescent years did not warrant the type of father she wanted in her present circumstance. She forgave him when she forgave herself.

While experiencing fatherlessness, Brandi always felt that she had to do more; she had to show her value. This is the source of her hardworking, tenacious, and career driven nature. She always felt like she had to prove herself and it shows in the woman she is today. Four days after graduating from a private university, she was in her field of work as an Art Director at a large Ad Agency, Team Detroit, in Michigan. She then transitioned from doing marketing work for this for-profit organization to doing the same at United Way for Southeastern Michigan, a nonprofit organization in Detroit. While working for the United Way, she realized that she did not wanted to have a larger impact in the personal development sector, so she started her business, ExpandFully LLC (also known as Expånd). Expånd is a life coaching and workshop facilitation company. Through Expånd, Brandi works with youth and young adults on understanding what their life's purpose and provides them with tools and resources for what they need to do to succeed and self-actualize. She also does freelance design work for her sole-proprietorship BeeKay Creative, in which she works with mission-based organizations to bring enhance the way they communicate visually. She hosts a monthly event called Toast2U which is an accomplishment and accountability party for women to celebrate their life milestones, and also set intentions to be held accountable for. She was recently nominated and is serving as Vice President for the Alumni of Challenge Detroit group. She is also a full-time admissions counselor at the College for Creative studies, a prestigious private art and design institution in Detroit. Usually as a fatherless daughter, you either seek to fill the void another man, or strengthen your self-sufficiency; Brandi did the latter. In her relationships, Brandi was always very guarded about the men she let into her space and never looked for a father figure in the men she chose to date. Her current guy, who is only the second boyfriend she has ever had, taught her how to love herself on a new level because of the way he loved her unconditionally. In her younger years, she also experienced familial issues with her paternal grandmother because of her mother and father's relationship. Brandi has begun to mend that relationship as well. Overall she is much better at addressing issues that may occur in her friendships or any other relationships because she learned how to build a relationship with her father.

Due to the combination of the good and bad of growing up fatherless, she is in a place where she has taken the good from the situation and allowed it to blossom, and taken the negative and uses it as soil to continue to her growth. Mentally, physically, and spiritually, she feels blessed and balanced. She feels whole. She doesn't feel like anything is missing. She has learned what self-love is and in her words, "I love myself, mind, body and spirit and that is a huge success."

Brandi's attributes her success to God. The advice that she would give to both young girls and women who are or have experienced fatherlessness is:

"The first this is forgiveness. Forgiveness sets you free from any situation, and forgiveness is giving up the chance for a better past. Forgiveness is the key to healing. The second thing is if you look at your life as a story, thinking about where you are right now, this is just your current chapter. Do not let where you are right now stop you from writing your story. Keep writing and keep working on your story. It doesn't have to end with, "I am a fatherless daughter, period."

Brandi experienced love, pain, and growth from growing up identifying with fatherlessness, but her growth has led to the development of a beautiful relationship with her father. Please know that it is never too late to grow, and it is never too late to build. A relationship is not based upon the length of time you have known a person, but it is based upon the strength of your foundation and the willingness to love through adversity..

Chapter Nine

What Determines True Success?

Being a Fatherless Daughter, there is sometimes a fear of being successful and it is primarily due to insecurities developed from not having a male figure in your life. Success is defined as the accomplishment of an aim or purpose. So based on this definition, the first step to success is to have an aim or purpose, and the second step is to accomplish it. The true aim and goal in life should be to be happy, and the main key is defining what happiness means to you. Most people, when they think of happiness, they think of money. I too used to believe this, but it is absolutely true what they say: "More money, potentially more problems." In order to determine what truly makes you happy, you must define your purpose. A lot of times, people don't usually determine their purpose until they are an adult and have lived and experienced life, but this is not the case for everyone. Below are some questions that should help you think about what your purpose is. The best part about these questions is that they are set up for you to go through the process of elimination, which will direct you closer to your purpose.

Name three things that you absolutely love to do.

1._____

2._____

3._____

Now of those three things, which two could you do for free and thoroughly enjoy?

1._____

2._____

Now of the two things listed above, which is something that you feel that you cannot leave this earth without doing?

1._____

Now let's analyze your last number one by asking one last question. Ask yourself, "Am I honoring God?" If you can honestly say, "Yes, I am," and there is scripture to validate, then congratulations, you are very close to finding your purpose. The last step is to pray and ask God to lead you to do His will. Keep in mind that this may not be revealed right away, but be diligent and stay prayerful and it will be shown.

Now that we have discussed purpose, lets discuss happiness because now you know what it takes to make you happy (operate in your purpose). Below is an activity that will help you to determine what truly makes you happy, and knowing what makes you happy will lead to success.

Here is a list of things that generally make people happy. Please write numbers 1-5 by each thing, not using one number more than once. These things will be listed by order of priority.

Money _____

Spirituality _____

Career _____

Education _____

Health _____

Now that you have listed in order of priority what makes you happy, below write why each thing is important to you.

Money

_____

_____

_____

_____

_____

Spirituality

_____
_____
_____
_____
_____
_____

Career

_____
_____
_____
_____

Education

_____
_____
_____
_____

Health

When writing your reasoning's down, you begin to put things into perspective. While all of these things are important, they hold different weight. Writing down why they are important prioritizes things for you. When you analyze your responses here and compare them to your purpose, things should start to make sense. For example, if your purpose is providing encouragement to people, then what you have determined makes you happy should be directly related. This is how you determine what true success is *for you*.

Chapter Ten

My Father In Heaven

The purpose of this book is to give you a different perspective on fatherlessness, and Kamilia's story is a somewhat different perspective than the other young women in this book. As we sat in Kamilia's office, she had tears of both joy and sadness as we discussed her biological father and her step daddy. Kamilia describes her relationship with her step-dad as being amazing. He stepped in and ended up being a great support system and a great influence in her life. She makes it clear that her stepdad was as much a father as any father can be, but when he got sick, she began her bout with fatherlessness. He could not be the active, outgoing force he once was, and that weight was heavy for both her and her mother. He passed a little over two years ago and she continues to celebrate his memory. Kamilia named her chapter, "My Father in Heaven" because both of her "Daddy's" are now in Heaven. Her stepdad passed in 2014 due to illness, and when her daddy went to heaven, she began to feel more of a presence from her spiritual Daddy. Kamilia was born and raised in the church (both her mother and stepdad were pastors), so she has always had a relationship with her spiritual Father, but the passing of her step-dad drew her closer.

Kamilia's Perspective

Up until Kamilia was eight years old, she was a Fatherless Daughter. Her biological father and mother were high school sweethearts, but at some point they realized that the relationship was not mutually beneficial, so they both agreed to part ways. During that time, Kamilia was too young to develop ill feelings, so she just adapted to what she was used to: being raised by her mother. She did ask herself questions that most young girls ask themselves who do not have their father, like, "why me?" or question why her father didn't want to be a part of her life, but Kamilia made a choice not to focus on what she did not have, and focus on what she did. Her mother was also very instrumental in instilling positivity and not disrespecting her father in anyway.

When Kamilia was eight, her mother was dating a guy who wanted to take her out for her birthday. Her mother told him that he had to ask Kamilia because she had been saving her money and was anticipating taking her out for her birthday. He went to Kamilia and asked her if he can take out both her and her mother for her mother's birthday. He even offered for Kamilia to keep her money and he pay for them both. Kamilia was so excited about keeping her money that she accepted the offer and that was the beginning to her "Daddy-Daughter" relationship. Her step-father and mother met in March and were married by May of the same year. They were married for eighteen years. The relationship that her and her stepdad built was comparable to none, so when he began to get sick, it was difficult for both her and her mother. She recalls when she was preparing to graduate from FAMU and thinking her step-dad would not be able to make it due to his illness. He had not travelled for at least ten years due to him being sick, and Kamilia was prepared for him not be able to come. When she got word that he was going to come, she was ecstatic. This was a big deal for her step-dad because when he was able to work, he was in show business, which means he travelled often. The fact that he was able to get on a plane and fly to see Kamilia walk across the stage meant the most to her.

As it relates to Kamila's relationship with her biological father, they had a really good friendship. Her parents broke up when she was a baby, and she did not meet her biological father until she was 22. He told her that he always wanted her and always loved her, but things just did not work out. At that moment, Kamilia accepted that and that was the beginning of their friendship. She loves the fact that she has gotten to know her siblings and his wife and has built and is continuing to build a loving relationship.

As Kamilia and I discussed her father and her stepfather, I noticed how she used the word "Daddy" when referencing her stepfather, and this prompted me to want to know her definition of a father versus a daddy. In her words, "A father is the husband, the provider, the enforcer and the reason you are here. daddy is love, and even when you say daddy, you are forced to smile. It is a term of endearment and positive connotations come along with it. Extra emotions are behind the word daddy. It's 'daddy little girl', not 'father's little girl'. A Daddy is a girl first love. There is an emotional difference. There are men out here who are great fathers, but may not be emotionally great fathers, and I think Daddy adds that emotional touch to it." Kamilia and I agree as it relates to Daddy versus Father, as I believe that with the word Daddy comes emotion. When you use the term, it comes natural and it is not something that you need to think about. How you feel is how you use it. By that I mean, if you have an emotional connection to your Father, you reference him as Daddy.

Kamilia's Trials

Kamilia learned at a young age to think positively and focus on what is. As stated previously, she asked herself questions about her biological father as a child, however, she adapted to the fact that he was not present in her life.

Authors Perspective

Acceptance is very important to the healing and dealing process and it can sometimes be difficult to do and takes time. Kamilia, with the aid of her mother, was able to accept her fatherless state very early on. At some point after asking herself questions about her father's whereabouts, she realized that he was not going to come home. She accepted it and continued to live her life. There is a lesson to be learned in this little girl learning what it means to accept. There is also a lesson in the 22-year-old girl who met her biological father for the first time and was able to heal and accept. While she may have felt some of the same emotions as any Fatherless Daughter, she chose not to allow it to affect her life.

Does Kamilia believe that if she had her biological father in her life, things would be different? Yes, she does. She talks about how she believes that she would have greater childhood memories. While the memories she has now are great, her stepdad became sick when she very young, so things such as traveling were things that they were unable to do. She also spoke about how she doesn't look at any experience as better or worst. As for having her biological father and her stepdad in her life, she believes that either circumstance would have shaped and molded how she views things now. What I found to be most interesting about this statement and what I get from the statement is God led her regardless of who was in her life. She is living a purposed life and it is one that God had for her, so she believes that all of her goals would have been accomplished, she may just have gotten to them differently.

Something else that we spoke about that almost all Fatherless Daughters experience is dating while fatherless. When Kamilia was in college and her dating life began, this was around the time her stepdad was sick and she had not yet developed a relationship with her biological father. While she states that she gained an immense amount of knowledge from her mother, she acknowledges that there are some things that a woman or a mother just cannot teach you and those are the things she relied on a father for.

Kamilia's Success

Kamilia defines success as achieving goals that you have set forth at a certain time in your life. At the young age of 27, Kamilia has achieved her goals and is constantly setting new goals to break through. She has graduated from high school, graduated from college and earned a Master's degree. She has the job that she loves, which is the Director of Programs and Membership Services for the National Association for the Advancement of Colored People. She also serves as third Vice President for the Michigan State Conference and Advisor of the Youth Council Detroit Branch NAACP. She has started her own businesses, one in which she is in partnership with another young lady and it is called the

GlassDrum. They specialize in project management and event planning. She is also in the process of starting her own décor and linen company, as this is something she has dabbled in for some time and she has decided to create a business, and she manages her mother's music career. She has a great relationship with her mother and a good friendship with her biological father. She attends church faithfully, has travelled extensively, had the opportunity to meet world class people and build relationships with people she would have never thought she would have access to. She has gained really great friendships with really great people, and all of these things are what success looks like to her. As one can clearly see, Kamilia has not and will not allow anything to stop her from being successful and achieving her goals. Kamilia has a very strong support system, but she ensures that she always puts God first, as he is her Savior and the reason she is who she is today. She also knows that while she can't see her stepdad, he is always there with her because she can feel him.

When asked what advice she would give to young girls and women who have identified with being fatherless, this is what she had to say: "Own it and Move on. Decide what it is that you want to do. If you want to identify yourself as fatherless, identify yourself that way, but don't let it halt you. It's so many other things to be in the world that are positive that I think it will hurt you to hold on to what you missed. It's a big world out there and within it, you can do anything. If you are holding on to the pain, and thinking about the tragedies in it and it is causing you to be upset, LET IT GO. Let it go, trust God, and move on. He (your father) may have only been here to give you life. That could have been the greatest gift he will ever give you. If he was in your life every day, you just may hate life, like there are so many possibilities of how things could have went. So accept what it is, whatever you choose to make it be, and then from there, be okay with it. Don't let it hurt you or halt you from reaching your highest potential. Just let it Go."

Chapter Eleven

Daddy's Girl...Still

While Tiffany was enjoying the Florida summer breeze and I was enjoying the Michigan summer heat, we discussed her recent experience with fatherlessness, and how it affected her life. Valentine's Day in 2011 was the last day that Tiffany spoke to her father, and he had only called her to wish her a happy Valentine's Day and to say he loved her. Little did she know that a few hours later, her uncle would be calling her to tell her that her Dad had gone home to be with the Lord. Tiffany is 28 years old, and did not experience fatherlessness until she was 23.

Tiffany was a self-proclaimed and everybody else-proclaimed "Daddy's Girl". She named her chapter, "Daddy's Girl...Still" because although her father is no longer with her in the physical, he is still with her in the spiritual and she is still a Daddy's Girl.

Tiffany's Perspective

Tiffany was born and raised in Detroit, MI, and while her parents were not together, she spent a lot of time with both of them. From as far back as she can remember, Tiffany was a Daddy's Girl, and what she can't remember, her immediate family does. She was always very close with her father, and she was even closer with him than she was with her mother. When there was a school problem, she called him. When there was a boy issue, she called him. When she needed new shoes, she called her dad. It was never a thought of hers that her father would not live long enough to see her first child.

Fast forward to Tiffany's adulthood. She still was spoiled by her father, but because she was so self-sufficient, he didn't always know when she was in need.

Like her dad and uncles, Tiffany got into the real estate business at a young age and she realized early on that real estate was something she wanted to make a career. Her dad and one of her uncles moved to south Florida, and her other uncle was on the way. While Tiffany had contemplated the move, her relationship at the time and her work kept her in Detroit. In late 2010 and early 2011, Tiffany dived head first into her work because that is when the real estate market was going through its transition and money was a little bit more difficult to come across.

Her father and one of his friends were playing around wrestling trying to determine who was stronger, and during the tussle, he injured his ankle. He thought that the injury was only a sprain and with time, it would heal. He flew to Detroit shortly after the scrimmage to visit family and friends. He ended up staying in Michigan for two weeks and while in Detroit, he realized his ankle wasn't feeling any better. He told his parents about what had happened and they urged him to go to the doctor.

Upon his visit, they determined that his ankle was broken, so they provided him pain medication and gave him permission to hop back on a plane to see his doctor in Florida. Tiffany was so into her work when her dad came to visit that she was too busy to see him, and only had a chance to speak with him via telephone once. When her dad returned home, he and his brother (Tiffany's uncle that also lived in South Florida) were moving into a different apartment. Also, Tiffany's other uncle and his girlfriend at the time were flying into Florida so that he could take his Real Estate Licensing Exam. On Valentine's Day, a few hours after she last spoke to her father, her uncle that had flew in called her multiple times, and initially she did not answer because she did not see his calls. Once she spoke to her uncle, he told her that her dad was being rushed to the hospital.

She was in a panic and did not know what to do, so she called her boyfriend at the time, and he did not answer. She cried and panicked until her uncle called her back at about 1 a.m. on February 15, 2011 to tell her that her father had passed away. The autopsy showed that her father died from a blood clot that had traveled to his lung. Had her father went to the doctor a little sooner and not been given permission to fly, it is very possible that he would still be on Earth today.

Tiffany's Trials

As one can only imagine, when you suddenly lose a parent, especially a parent that has been active in your life, you lose a portion of yourself. Even dealing with this as an adult, this can still be a tough pill to swallow. When her dad passed, she was so busy being a rock to others, she forgot to grieve for herself. When you don't grieve in a timely manner, this can cause for mental exhaustion and a physical explosion. After he passed, Tiffany went through a time of not working, or doing anything. She felt the guilt of not seeing him when he was in town before his death because she was working too much, so she took time off work. During this time, she grieved and became intentional about spending time with family.

The Authors Perspective

In a previous chapter, I spoke on how fatherlessness prepares you for life's trials. As you see above and you will see below, Tiffany's tribulations prepared her for what was to come in her life. It taught her the importance of time and how she should better utilize it. It taught her a different aspect of love. Essentially, it taught her how to be the best wife, the best mother, the best friend, the best daughter to Christ, and the best to those in need.

Tiffany's trials actually created testimony. What she went through, losing her parent, made her stronger and made her better. Shortly after her father passing and her grieving, she did what she believed was best for her life and moved to South Florida with her uncles. Not too long after moving there, she met the man that would become her husband. When they first started dating, she saw so much of her father in him, and this helped her to close the gap and gain some closure. When they married, she was deliberate about spending time. She made sure she set aside time specifically for her husband.

It was when she became pregnant that she owned the fact that she was fatherless. It was at that time she realized that her child would not experience the physical life of her grandfather. Something amazing that happened for her though, is she began to realize that her father was with her in spirit once she got married. She and her husband married in St. Thomas, and there is a picture that's shows a light behind her. What was weird to her is that she took many pictures in the same spot, but only one shows the light. There is also a picture with her and her daughter that shows the same light. Tiffany finds comfort in knowing that her father is with her.

Tiffany's Success

Success to Tiffany is mental growth. She believes that you cannot become successful until you learn to control your mind. While she is a 28-year-old woman, she recognizes that she is still growing, but her continuous growth comes from her experiences and how she handles them. Tiffany is a wife, a mother, a daughter, a sister, a niece, and a friend. These are all successes in her eyes. She is also a successful entrepreneur. Tiffany has been working in real estate since 2007, and that has been her primary source of income. She is licensed in both Michigan and Florida, and she specializes in relocation, buyer's agent, listing agent, and property management. She and her husband have also owned multiple other businesses, and they currently run a nonprofit. The nonprofit is called Kid Power Play Sports, and the objective is to assist children in becoming healthy by implementing sport activities. It also covers the importance of nutrition and promoting mental, spiritual, and physical health. As a part of Kid Power Play Sports, they have a football camp that hosts different classes to aid in a healthier lifestyle.

As Tiffany and I were wrapping up our interview, I asked if there was any advice that she would like to give to women who may have experienced what she did, or even young girls who are fatherless.

"To young girls and adult women, I would say to know that this too shall past. Know that every life experience that happens is for a reason and we all have the ability to tap into a greater self."

Chapter Twelve

God Has Already Determined Your Success

"For you created my inmost being; you knit me together in my mothers womb. I praise you because I am fearfully and wonderfully made; your works are wonderful, I know that full well. My frame was not hidden from you when I was made in the secret place, when I was woven together in the depths of the earth. Your eyes saw my unformed body; all the days ordained for me were written in your book before one of them came to be." Psalms 139: 13-16 (NIV)

Do you honestly, truly, and whole heartedly believe this? If so, you know that you were put on this earth for purpose on purpose. You know that you have a gift that God has given you specifically. You know that the gift He has provided you will lead to the true desires of your heart. You know that God did not intend sadness or sorrow for any of us, even though we have a father who helped create us, but maybe didn't help raise us or left us too soon. When you truly understand this, you know that regardless of your fatherless perspective, you are still made to be successful. Listening to God isn't always easy, but it must be done in order for you to determine what your God-given gift is. You must also learn to use all five senses to listen to God. You have to pay attention to what you see, hear, touch, smell, and taste. This may sound weird, but if your gift is cooking, then you have to at some point utilize all of your senses to determine this.

The true definition of success, in my opinion, is pure bliss. What defines happiness for you may not be happiness for me, so that is when you have to dig down to the root of your happiness. For example, most people believe that money aids in their happiness. When someone believes this, the question is HOW does money make you happy? This is where the digging begins and you start to say, "money makes me happy because…" Once you question the because, the true reason why you are happy comes to light. You realize that it is not because of the money that you are happy, but what the money allows you to do. Someone may say that money makes them happy because it allows them to provide for their family. The true happiness is being able to provide for their family, not the money.

"For we are God's handiwork, created in Christ Jesus to do good works, which God prepared in advance for us to do." Ephesians 2:10 (NIV)

God knew we were great before we were conceived. He made us that way. Let's not use our trials as a crutch, but let's use them as testimonies. When you see someone else make it through the storm, it encourages you, it inspires you, and it empowers you to make it through the storm as well. It also influences you to share your testimony and be a blessing to someone else.

Chapter Thirteen

I Was Always Hopeful

At the very young age of 22, Jessika has accomplished so much and still on the road to accomplish more, and she has done this all without her biological father physically present. Jessika's mother was in a car accident when she was ten years old, and prior to this, her father was barely in her life. When the accident happened, her aunt (his sister) contacted her father and told him that he needed to step up and be a father, and he said that he would. He went to pick Jessika up and took her to the mall and she was so excited. While they were on the way to grab some food, his wife called, and he asked Jessika to be quiet because he did not want his wife to know that he was with his daughter. This is the moment that a young Jessika came to the realization that she was fatherless.

Jessika's Perspective

Jessika suffered from lack of trust and lack of affection due to not having a father or a father figure in her life. There were many times that her father said that he would be there for her, but wasn't. She never received affection or her definition of love from him, so she struggled with how to show and give love and affection.

The Authors Perspective

This is something that many fatherless women struggle with. We do not know how to love because we believe that our father did not love us. He did not love us enough to stay. He did not love us enough to be there. He did not love us enough to care. We use that as an excuse to be women that are not of love, but are of hate, frustration, sadness, and depression. My motto is if you can physically say out of your mouth, "I am this way because I did not have my father," then it is something that you can change. As stated several times in this book, manifestation is real. Your thoughts and what you say can become your reality, so be careful of the seeds you plant. You want flowers to bloom, not dead roots to sprout.

Jessika's father was never a part of her life, primarily because he is a married to a woman that wants him to have nothing to do with anyone outside of their family unit, including his daughter, Jessika. Jessika yearned for her father to be a part of her life, and has asked for him to be several times, but he was never willing. The reason she named her chapter, "I was Always Hopeful," is because even when her father dismissed her multiple times, she was always hopeful that he would come around and start being a father. Jessika's father is still married to the same woman, which means she is still struggling to build a relationship with him, but according to her, she is still open to seeing where the relationship can go.

Jessika's Trials

Jessika has had to deal with fatherlessness all of her life, and did not become accepting of it until she was an adult and got to college. In May of 2015, she was getting ready to graduate from college and she contacted her father and asked that he be there. At this time, her mother was unable to attend and she wanted one of her parents to support her at her graduation. When she contacted him, he told her that he was unable to attend because his wife would not allow. At this point in her life, she had matured and developed an understanding of her father's patterns. She knew that as long as his wife had a say so, it would be difficult to build a relationship.

Her father not being there caused a lot of emotional issues which often times caused her to shut off from the world. She has lost several friends because of her nonchalant attitude w-hich was derived from her believing that because her father wasn't there for her, her friends wouldn't be either. It took her all of her teenage life to fight through this, and what she had to realize was the reason she was this way. Once she understood the reason, she was able to be present, learned to channel her energy, and worked on self-building.

Jessika's Success

Jessika defined success as being passionate and able to truly love what you do. She also stated that to be successful is to be happy. Through all that she has been through with her father, being able to self-build and self-educate has become extremely important to her. She is very deliberate about the seeds that she plants, how she feeds them, and how they grow. This is also a reason that she is successful. She has learned to control what she thinks and what she manifests. Communication and being able to effectively communicate is a form of success to Jessika. There was a point in time where Jessika did not care to hear what anyone had to say, and she did not listen. Not only did she not listen, but she barely talked either. She is now able to hear what people have to say and also communicate her points effectively.

Aside from Jessika's emotional success, she has also had academic and professional success. She holds two bachelor's degrees, one in Kinesiology Exercise Science and the other in Business Administration with a focus in Marketing. Not only does she hold two degrees at the age of twenty-two, but she holds those degrees with honors. Jessika also started her own cosmetic line called

JusCouture, which is cruelty free and 100% vegan, when she was just eighteen and she is still in operation and looking to expand. She has also opened, managed, and maintained a boutique, and she is currently in school pursuing her esthetician license. Jessika is also the founder of a nonprofit organization called Phase 2 Girls. She feels that as a young girl, she did not always have someone to talk to other than her mother or grandmother, so that is why Phase 2 Girls was created. The purpose of the organization is to provide young girls with a mentor and a big sister. When Jessika was asked about the advice she would provide to young girls and young women on how to cope with fatherlessness, she said, "Do not seek the love of a father through a man. Do not allow yourself to [feel the void] of not having a father and seek it in a man. Focus on yourself and building yourself up, and find it within yourself to forgive him."

Chapter Fourteen

The Heart Of A Legacy, Mind Over Matter (The Doctor's Perspective)

For this book, I thought that it was very imperative to get a doctor's perspective, and a doctor who works with children who are fatherless or have experienced fatherlessness. Dr. Kim Login-Nowlin was gracious enough to provide her expert opinion. Because these are words of a psychiatric professional, none of her words have been paraphrased.

Dr. Kim Logan-Nowlin Biography

Kim Logan Communications Christian Counseling Clinic has been successfully addressing the needs of families, youth and individuals experiencing problems, or those with marital concerns, by providing family therapy, child therapy, and substance abuse treatment. KLCC has provided employability training and substance abuse treatment to parole and probationary offenders since 1993.

For twenty-eight years, Dr. Kim Logan- Nowlin has treated and trained people from all walks of life. She continues to serve the community through consistent support and is committed to the concerns of individuals and families experiencing problems which prevent a healthy lifestyle.

This includes the areas of Parenting, Divorce, Adoption, and children of incarcerated parents. Kim Logan Communication is an international professional motivational speaker/lecturer for family life. Kim Logan Communications Clinic provides an afterschool mentoring program, and drama troop. KLCC also provides a husband and wife team perspective for our couples and families. Arthur E. Nowlin LMSW, CAACD,

AAFLP. Dr. Logan-Nowlin, is also a member of ACA & APA.

Dr. Kim's Perspective

During my formative years growing up after my parents divorced, it was still made very apparent that my father would remain a constant positive figure in my life. He continued to provide support to my mother and offer his skills where they were needed for all the children within our family structure.

Being an absent parent does not always represent the component of love. Spiritual and educational guidance, and strength will be absent also. My father was not in the home, but he was not an absent father. My father equipped me with the ability to strive, and taught me that nothing was out of reach for me.

My parents wanted me to become accomplished, independent, and never depend on myself, but put all my trust in God. Both my parents gave me their hearts of love, and that provided me with a legacy to love my husband, children, and others. My mother taught me excuses only get in your way and if "there is a will, there is a way."

I implemented different affirmations into this response from my book "The Legacy of Love" that "leaning back only breaks your back" and I'm pressing forward. We can't change our past, but we can learn from it.

I have also implemented my own theory of adapting and adjusting to some of the missing elements that I experienced after my parents' divorce, and it is called "Mind Over Matter Theory". It discusses having an attitude of excellence and excelling with determined levels of competence.

This, along with the legacy from my parents, extended family, church, community village, educational leaders, and mentors empowered me to have standards that first please God and allows me to know my purpose of action in this life. This allowed me to also filter the negative and retain the positive, and to be an asset and not a liability to my family legacy.

1. Children within nuclear families have to cope with transitions, family environment, and individual attitude to assist them in family formation and positive functioning skills just like children from single parenting household. All children must adjust to their own family origins and how they fit into the scope of their own reality.

   The nuclear family child has to conceptualize his/her difference by the challenges that are presented within a two parent household, and process information that will help them handle any situation that may be presented to them. This does not diminish the exemplary efforts of many single parents, whose courage and determination has directed their children to become successful.

2. In relation to the success of a child being in a fatherless home, we can take a close look at President Barak Obama and Dr. Ben Carson, who were both raised without their

fathers. The motive, in my opinion, can't be driven by a hidden agenda to prove oneself. That is totally exhausting and it accomplishes absolutely nothing from the framework of creating a healthy outlook of one's life. Inspiration can't be diminished by one's own effort to self-medicate a void that can only be filled with love for self, appreciation for mankind and a true devotion to God. Any person given the right tools and genuine support can strive towards excellence. A single parent home should not define or derail you. Therefore, never allow any person situation to limit your outcome.

3. Some common issues I see in fatherless children is a need to be loved and accepted by their peers. Difficulty developing life skills, unable to comply with the law and authority, isolation, deprived of love, direction and inferiority complex. People develop an inferiority complex when they find themselves different in a way that affects their self-worth. If the child believed that not having a father makes him less worthy than others, then

there is a strong possibility that the child will develop an inferiority complex.

4. When a child is a victim of circumstances beyond their control the outcome presents a different framework. The child had their father within the home structure since birth.

They were given the balance of two parents and saw a glimpse of having an established foundation. When a person decided to raise a child alone or is put in a situation that caused them to alter their lives (incarceration, death, rape) then one has to recognize how to re-align themselves to be a change agent for themselves and their child. Being a parent is difficult, whether there are two parents or just one.

But each parent is required to be a constant support so that the child will make the best decision that they can for their future.

A two parent income home provides less hardship, but the three key components remain regardless: balance, integrity, and self-respect, to empower a child to duplicate high standards from his/ her parents. This can also apply to a single parent but they will need the extension of a positive village more so to provide assistance to the child. Not to say a two parent child would not benefit from the extended village also.

5. In giving advice to a child at the onset of counseling, I would try to gain as much information as I could to help prepare and structure for a healthy relationship for her. As a behavioral therapist I would implement art and music therapy to develop untapped skills that could become a positive reinforcement in child therapy. Also, establishing or re-establishing the trust factor. The child needs to have a comfort level to trust their surroundings to have desire to make an effort to change for the positive.

Help the child to remember the good in their lives in order to use it as a building block of strength. In adult women they must learn to face their feelings with honesty. They must learn that these feelings are their own and they must express them in tangible, creative and safe environment.

Don't allow others to tell you how you feel. Learn to take care of your health and be aware of your triggers that may cause a relapse in therapy or having a productive life.

Authors Perspective

Dr. Kim made several great points, as her many years of expertise and education affords her to do so. She answered one of the questions stating that the agenda cannot be to prove oneself, as that alone accomplishes nothing.

I agree that that alone accomplishes nothing, but that desire along with a driving force of motivation can absolutely propel you into full speed of success.

Many fatherless daughters start off having this very thought and this thought can manifest into something great depending on what you do with this thought. It is all about changing the negative to a positive. The thought alone is negative, but what it has the ability to do can be extremely positive.

Overall, Dr.Kim's thorough analysis is one that provides a perspective that you may only get from a professional. Her experience matters and is the reason children and adults learn to cope with situations that are out of their control.

Chapter Fifteen

You Are The Daughter Of A King

Our **Father**, who art in Heaven, hallowed be thy name, thy kingdom come…

God is your Father, even if you have a father physically present. As I wrap up Fatherless Daughter: A Different Perspective, I want you to be cognizant of your Creator, the Almighty, the Alpha and Omega, the one we now call and know as Jesus. He is the Way, the Truth and the Life, and when and where we fall short in life, He is always there to pick you up. Statistics state the following about fatherless children:

In the United States 23.9 million children live absent of their biological fathers. Fatherless children represent:

- 63% of teen suicides
- 70% of juveniles in state institutions
- 71% of high school drop outs
- 75% of children in chemical abuse centers
- 80% of rapists
- 85% of youth in prison
- 90% of homeless and runaway children[4]

While these statistics may hold true, there are several statistics that have not been reported about children experiencing fatherlessness. Many of us have not been in state institutions, are not high school dropouts, are not rapists or in chemical abuse centers, have not been to prison, homeless, or runaways. The primary reason for this is because of our Father in heaven who has been

---

[4] Parentless Statistics via FCLU.org

protecting us and keeping us out of harm's way. It is also thanks to those who raised us, sometimes it was a village, and sometimes it was a single mother. We need to honor those who are a part of our success and who believed in us. Because of them, we are who we are.

Over the last several months of conducting research to complete this book, I have been fortunate enough to meet a few awesome men and women who are fatherless or who have identified with being fatherless in their lives. The purpose of this project is to shed light on a few of those who I have encountered, and who are willing to share their story.

I could not close this book without an activity to help you realize who you truly are. The first thing I would like for you to do is to identify your values. Values are things that are important to you and important to the way you live. There are a few steps that you can take to identify your values.

1. Think about times when you were the happiest. What were you doing and what contributed to your happiness? (You want to think about times from your personal and professional life)

2. Recall some times in your life when you were most satisfied. What need or desire was filled, and why did the experience give your life meaning?

3. Now, think about what your dream career would be? This may require you to think back to when you were a child.

Now that you have followed these steps, take a look of some common core values and choose your top five (if your values are not on the list, you can still list them)

Achievement	Ambition	Balance	Boldness	Challenge	Cheerful
Commitment	Community	Compassion	Consistency	Courtesy	Creativity
Dependability	Determination	Diligence	Discipline	Economy	Effectiveness
Empathy	Equality	Excellence	Expressiveness	Fairness	Faith
Family	Fitness	Freedom	Generosity	Growth	Happiness
Hard work	Honesty	Humility	Independence	Intelligence	Joy
Justice	Leadership	Love	Loyalty	Making a difference	Obedience
Patriotism	Positivity	Professionalism	Reliability	Self-actualization	Self-reliance
Serenity	Service	Simplicity	Stability	Strength	Structure
Success	Teamwork	Time	Tradition	Trustworthiness	Unity
Vision					

1. _____

2. _____

3. _____

4. _____

5. _____

The next thing I want you to think about is your personal mission statement. A personal mission statement is simply a statement that defines who you are, and what your purpose is on this Earth. The key to writing this statement is to make sure that it aligns with your values that you listed above. After pondering for a few moments, write out your personal mission statement below. This may require you to do some research on others personal mission statement to give you an idea on how to draft your own. (If you need more space, please refer to the notes section in the back of this book.)

_____

_____

_____

_____

_____

_____

_____

_____

So now that you have discovered your values and personal mission statement, you should now have a clear idea of who you are and whose you are. You were put here on purpose with a purpose and that came from your Daddy who sits on a thrown above the skies. Understanding this helps you to focus less on statistics and on the negatives and focus more on yourself personally and your growth. It is sometimes easy to get caught up on what society says that you are, but with the knowingness of your ability and capability, you can do anything and you can be anything. Regardless of the fact that you are fatherless or have identified with fatherless, I, A. Morel Brown want you to know one important thing…

"I can do all things through Christ who strengthens me." Philippians 4:13 (NKJV)

Acknowledgements

I would first and foremost like to thank my Spiritual Father, for it is He who has strategically placed perfect purpose within me. Because of Him, I am able to use my gifts to be a blessing to others, and that is something that I will never be able to thank Him for enough.

I would like to thank my mother, Angela Johnson. It is because of her prayers, because of her faith, and because of her strength and relationship with God that I have grown into the woman I have become today. She is not only my mother, but my best friend forever! This may seem odd, but I would also like to thank my father. While he was not and is not active in life, he is partly the reason I am able to operate in purpose, and it is because of him that FDADP was born. I am who I am because of God first, and both my parents second.

I would like to thank the women who are a part of this book: Nicole, Brandi, Kamilia, Tiffany, Jessika, and Dr. Kim Logan-Nowlin. If not for you and your bravery in sharing your stories, this book project would not be what it is. I especially want to thank Brandi Keeler for her amazing support from beginning to end.

Thank you Roselyn Paride for formatting the book.

Thanks you to all of the young women I have mentored within the past few years. Your stories have inspired me to want to share mines and I want you all to know that there is strength in your story. Lastly, I want to thank all of my family and friends for all of your support. I have so many text messages, social media messages, and emails of encouragement that I often look back at to push me forward. I love you all!

#IAmFatherlessBut

Are you a fatherless daughter, BUT you have forgiven and overcome? What methods did you use to forgive and how did you overcome? What is success to you and what are your successes? To share your story for a chance to be featured on social media or AMorelBrown.com, please email: hello@amorelbrown.com

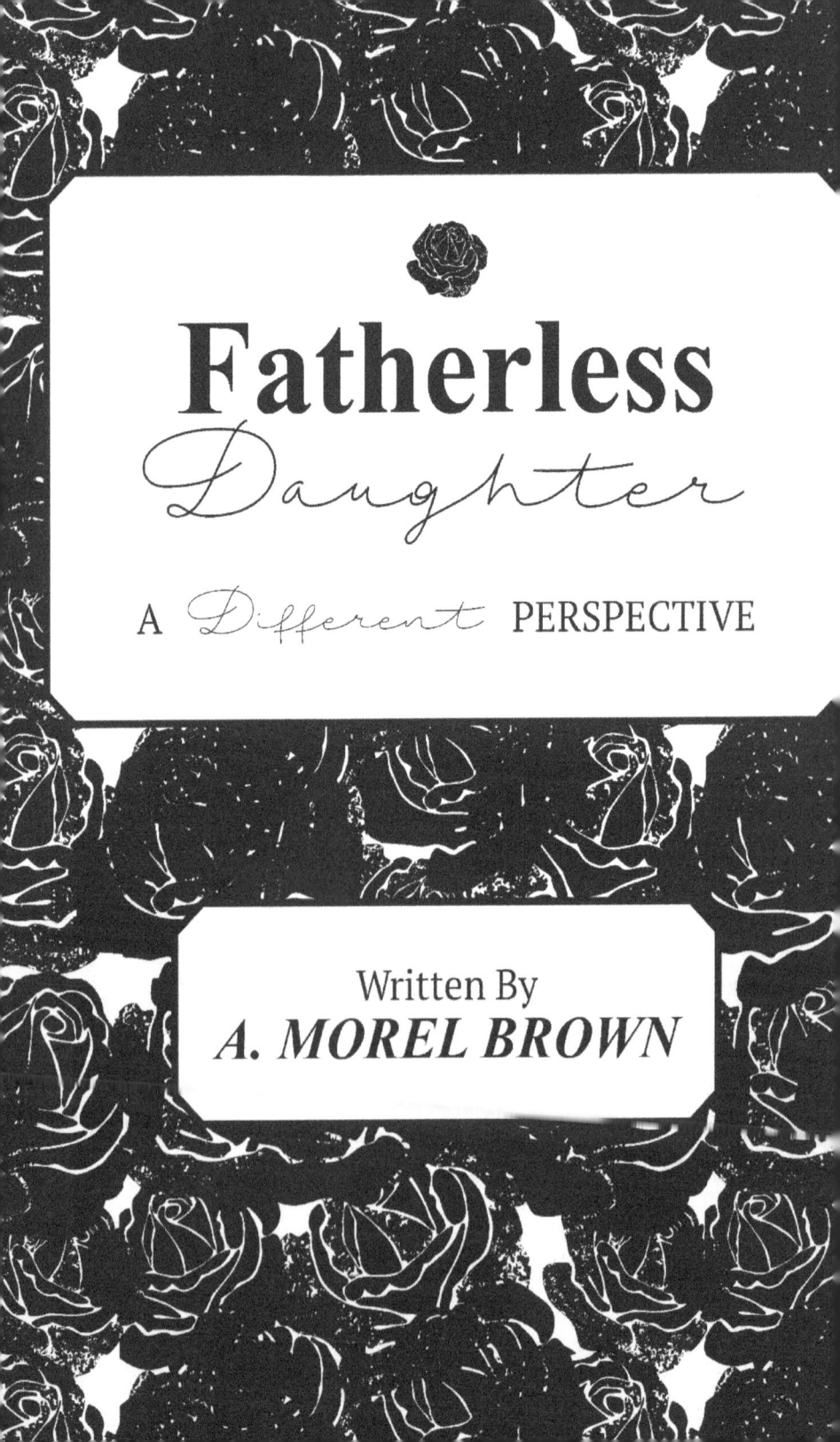

www.ingramcontent.com/pod-product-compliance
Lightning Source LLC
Chambersburg PA
CBHW031134090426
42738CB00008B/1084